Common Core I

I

By C

Published by Gallopade International, Inc.
©Carole Marsh/Gallopade
Printed in the U.S.A. (Peachtree City, Georgia)

TABLE OF CONTENTS

G: Includes Graphic Organizer
GO: Graphic Organizer is also available 8½" x 11" online
   download at www.gallopade.com/client/go
(numbers above correspond to the graphic organizer numbers online)

What Is Light?

Read the text and answer the questions.

When you wake up in the morning, is it daylight? Does the sunlight help you get up and start your day? Or, when you wake up, is it still dark? Do you use electricity to turn on lights in your house so you can see your way to brush your teeth, get dressed, eat breakfast, and start your day?

Where would we be without light? In the dark! We can't see light directly, but light is the reason we can see!

What is light? Light is a form of energy. Light comes from a source object, usually a very hot object like the sun. The sun is a natural source of visible light, radio waves, infrared radiation, and many other energy waves. These waves are all part of a type of energy called the electromagnetic <u>spectrum</u>. What we call light, or visible light, is the only part of the spectrum we can see!

Light waves are not all the same. They can be brighter or duller. They can produce any of the colors of the rainbow, as well as white, and in a round-about way, they help produce black. Light waves are essential in order for us to detect everything we see. Have you ever imagined life without light? Luckily, we don't have to!

1. Use the text to list four facts about light.

2. Use the text to explain the relationship between light and light waves.

3. Use the text to explain the relationship between light and the electromagnetic spectrum.

4. Use the text to explain the relationship between light and the sun.

5. According to the text, how do we see light?

6. A. Use a dictionary to define <u>spectrum.</u>
   B. What inference would you make about the electromagnetic spectrum based on the definition of the word <u>spectrum</u>?

7. Think about how light affected you yesterday. Write a journal entry describing some of the ways you encountered light. How was it useful? How did it make you feel? What would you do without it?

A Railway Station

Look at the photograph and answer the questions.

Courtesy of Wikipedia

1. What is the mood of this photograph? How do light and dark elements help create this mood?

2. Why can you see some parts of this photograph and not others?

3. What is a source of light in this photograph?

4. Predict what this picture would look like without light.

5. What is the relationship between light and sight? Explain.

6. Make 3 inferences about light from this photograph. Support each inference with details from the text.

Sources of Light

Complete the graphic organizer by identifying several sources of light that surround your everyday life.

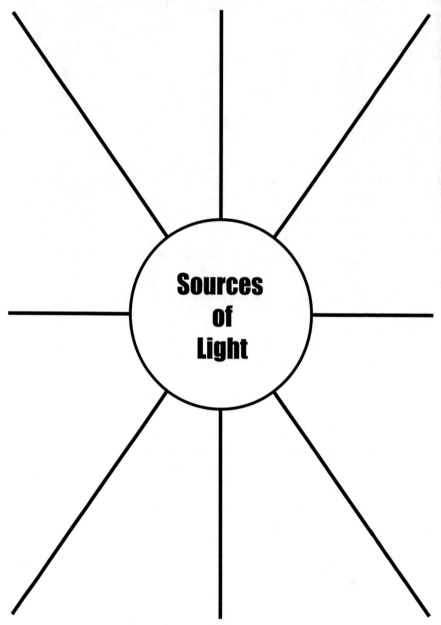

Sources of Light

Light in the Sky

Read the text and answer the questions.

The universe is a big place. But the sun is already very familiar. You can see the sun in the sky and feel its heat, even though it is approximately 93 million miles away from Earth. Energy from the sun warms the Earth, brings daylight, and affects weather around the world. In fact, life on Earth would not be possible without the light from the sun. Plants need the sun's light energy to grow.

Light is the fastest particle in the universe, traveling through space at 186,000 miles per second. Even at such a high speed, it takes sunlight about 8 minutes to reach Earth.

Approximately 239,000 miles from the Earth, the moon is the brightest light in the night sky. The moon's brightness often makes it difficult to see many of the stars in the sky. The moon, however, does not produce light by itself. The moon's surface actually reflects white light from the sun!

On a clear, moonless night, the skies are spotted with starlight. Distant stars in other solar systems produce light that travels huge distances through space. The closest star to Earth, other than the sun, is Alpha Centauri. Alpha Centauri is approximately 4.37 light years from Earth. A "light year" is the distance light travels in 1 year. Stars are so far away, the starlight we see today could have come from a star that no longer exists!

1. What is the Earth's primary source of natural light?

2. Identify at least three ways the sun's light energy affects the Earth.

3. A. How long does it take for light to reach the Earth from the sun?
    B. Approximately how long does it take moonlight to reach the Earth from the moon?
    C. Estimate when the moonlight you see was created.

4. Why is a "clear, moonless night" ideal for viewing stars?

5. If Alpha Centauri exploded today, when would we see a change in the night sky?

Light in Motion

Read the text and answer the questions.

In ancient times, scientists studied light by <u>observation</u>. They watched carefully and noticed facts about light. Scientists long ago knew light somehow traveled through the air, because they saw that light, when blocked by an object, created a shadow. But, they could not explain what light was made of or how it moved.

Now, scientists know that light is made of tiny particles called photons. Each photon is a tiny packet of light energy. Photons of light travel together in an up-and-down wave motion.

Unlike sound waves that spread out as they travel, light waves travel in a straight line called a <u>ray</u>. The knowledge that light rays only travel in a straight line explains how shadows work. When an object blocks the straight path of light rays, it creates a shadow.

Sound waves require a medium, such as air or water, to travel through, but light waves do not. Light can travel through the vacuum of space. In space, light travels about 186,000 miles per second—the fastest speed in the universe! However, when light passes through a medium, such as air, water, or glass, the waves slow down and become longer.

1. A. Define <u>observation</u> as it is used in the text.
   B. What "tool" did ancients scientists use to observe light?

2. Compare and contrast what ancient scientists knew about light with what scientists know today.

3. Explain the relationship of photons to light.

4. What motion does light make as it travels?

5. List at least two ways a light wave is different from a sound wave.

6. A. Define <u>ray</u> as it is used in the text.
   B. Use the text to draw a diagram illustrating how light rays create a shadow.

EXPERIMENT

Transparent, Opaque, & Translucent

Read the text and conduct the experiment by shining a flashlight directly on each object. Then complete the table and answer the questions.

> Light can pass through many types of solids, liquids, and gases. However, light cannot pass through all objects.
>
> When light can pass through an object, the object is called transparent. When light cannot pass through an object, the object is called opaque. When some light passes through an object, but not all of it, the object is called translucent.

Object	Describe it	Test it	Conclusion
Construction paper	Solid, thick paper; colored	Light did not pass through the paper	Construction paper is opaque.
Tissue paper			
Plastic wrap			
Clear glass			
Plastic lid			
Cardboard box			
Wax paper			
Aluminum foil			
Paper towel			
Wood			

1. What are common characteristics of opaque objects?

2. What are common characteristics of transparent objects?

3. How does a translucent object affect light passing through it?

Wavelength and Amplitude

Read the text and answer the questions.

> For centuries, people have watched the ocean and observed waves rise and fall. To better study waves, scientists named the parts of a wave. Many of the same terms used to describe ocean waves and other mechanical waves (such as sound waves) are used to describe light waves.
>
> The highest point of a wave is called a <u>crest</u>. The lowest point of a wave is called the <u>trough</u>. A wave rises and falls, or crests and troughs, many times as it moves.
>
> <u>Amplitude</u> is the height of a wave. The height of a wave is measured from the center of a wave to its highest point (crest), or lowest point (trough). Amplitude provides information about the intensity of a light. When a light wave carries high amplitude, the light has more energy and is very bright. When a light has low amplitude, it is soft and dull.
>
> <u>Wavelength</u> is the distance between two crests, or two high points of a wave. For light waves, wavelength provides information about the kind of light produced by the wave. The light we can see has wavelengths between about 400 nanometers and 700 nanometers. Each color of light has a different wavelength. Red has the longest wavelength and violet has the shortest wavelength.

1. Use the text to label each part of the wave:
    A. crest   B. wavelength   C. trough   D. amplitude

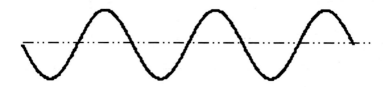

2. A. How does a light wave's wavelength affect the light we see?
    B. How does a light wave's amplitude affect the light we see?

3. Predict how each of the following lights would look.
    A. low amplitude; longest light wavelength
    B. high amplitude; shortest light wavelength

Colors of the Visible Spectrum

Read the text and chart, and answer the questions.

The <u>visible spectrum</u> is all the colors of light the human eye can see, including red, orange, yellow, green, blue, and violet. Each color of light has a different wavelength. Wavelength determines what color of light we see.

"White light" is the most common light we see every day. White light comes from the sun, fire, light bulbs, and other sources. However, the name "white light" is misleading. White light is actually a combination of all colors of light. That means white light contains all wavelengths of visible light! Light from the sun, a fire, or a light bulb appears white because it contains all colors of the visible spectrum. If you break white light into its different wavelengths, you will see a rainbow of all colors.

1. A. Use the text to define <u>visible spectrum</u>.
   B. Explain the connection between visible spectrum and wavelength.

2. Why is the term "white light" misleading?

3. A. Look for a pattern in the chart, and describe it.
   B. Use the pattern to estimate the wavelength for the color orange.

Color	Wavelength
red	620-750 nm
orange	
yellow	570-590 nm
green	495-570 nm
blue	450-495 nm
violet	380-450 nm

4. Each wave below belongs to a color of the visible spectrum. Use the color/wavelength chart to label each wave.

5. A. What is the longest wavelength of light we can see?
   B. What is the shortest wavelength of light we can see?

Reflection

Read the text and answer the questions.

What happens when light waves strike an object? The answer depends on what the object is, and how flat or rough the surface of the object is. Sometimes, light waves hit an object and bounce back. When a light wave bounces off an object, it is called <u>reflection</u>.

Objects that are flat, shiny, and smooth often reflect light at the same angle it hits. Think about a smooth, flat surface like a mirror or a flat lake. On a mirror, light rays bounce back at the same angle they hit. This is how you can see yourself reflected on the surface of a mirror or flat lake.

On the other hand, rough and dull objects reflect light, but they scatter it in all directions. Think about rough brick—you can't see yourself reflected in a brick! Curved surfaces like a funhouse mirror reflect light in different directions, too, causing the reflected image to twist or distort.

If all surfaces were flat and shiny, we could not see the actual objects we look at. Rough and dull objects allow us to see an object, including its shape, size, and color because it is not evenly reflecting all of the light from other objects around it.

1. Use the text to define <u>reflection</u>.

2. How does the surface of an object affect the reflection of light?

3. A. What words would you use to describe reflective objects?
   B. Give three examples of items that reflect light.

4. A. What words would you use to describe objects that scatter light?
   B. Give three examples of objects that scatter light.

5. Use the text to draw lines illustrating how light rays will reflect off these two surfaces.

Colors: Absorbed & Reflected

Read the text and answer the questions.

"White light" is the combination of all wavelengths of visible light (ROYGBV). The sun, light bulbs, and candles all produce white light.

When waves of white light strike an object, some wavelengths of light are absorbed, or taken in, and other wavelengths are reflected, or bounced off. The reflected wavelengths are what the human eye sees as color.

Imagine a green apple. Why does the apple look green? When white light strikes the apple, the apple absorbs all wavelengths of the visible spectrum, except green! Green is the only color wavelength reflected by the apple. Therefore, when the reflected light enters the human eye, the apple looks green.

What about the color black? When talking about light, black is not a color. Black is the absence of light. When an object absorbs all wavelengths of light, and reflects none, it looks black.

1. Make inferences from the text to complete the chart.

Object	Absorbed colors	Reflected colors
shiny red sports car		
lemon		
lime		
grape soda		
your shirt		

2. What is the relationship between wavelength and color?

3. Use the text to draw a diagram illustrating how light waves allow us to see colors.

4. What colors does a white sheet of paper absorb? What colors does it reflect? Explain your response using logic and evidence from the text.

Light

Complete the graphic organizer by identifying sources, characteristics, and effects of light.

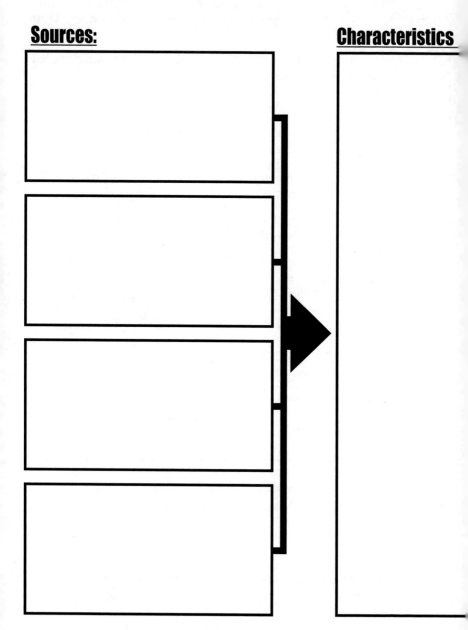

Sources:

Characteristics

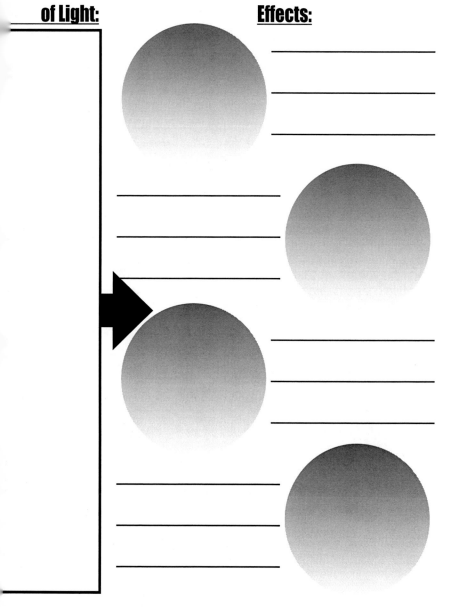

of Light:

Effects:

Why Is the Sky Blue?

In small groups, do the research and writing prompts.

PART A: Make a list of things you know about light and color. Include definitions for reflection, absorption, and wavelength. Include an explanation of what you observe when you see light and color, and why.

PART B: Make a list of things you know about the light you see when you look at the sky during the daytime. Based on where that light comes from and what you know about that light, what color would you expect the sky to be? Why?

> *For centuries, people have asked the question, "Why is the sky blue?" The answer lies in what happens when light passes through the earth's atmosphere.*

PART C: Make a list of things you know or think/guess about the Earth's atmosphere. Identify which things on your list you know vs. which ones you are not sure about.

PART D: Use the information you have compiled to write a hypothesis answering the question, "Why is the sky blue?"

PART E: Discuss each group's hypothesis as a class. If desired, revise your hypothesis based on new insight from the discussion.

PART F: Use an online resource to research why the sky is blue. Then answer the following questions.

1. Use your research to write an explanation of why the sky is blue.

2. Compare and contrast your hypothesis with the actual explanation you learned in your research. Was your hypothesis similar to the actual explanation for why the sky is blue?

3. Write an essay expressing the opinion that "sharing knowledge is important to science." Use the process you went through in this activity to support your opinion. Cite specific examples.

Refraction

Read the text and answer the questions.

Have you ever noticed that a straw looks bent in your drink? This bending is a trick of light called <u>refraction</u>. Refraction is simply light's change in direction between mediums. The straw *looks* bent underwater because the light is refracted in a different direction than when it travels through the air.

Refraction is caused by a change in the speed of light. In space, where there is no medium, light travels at 186,000 miles per second—the fastest speed in the universe! But when light enters the Earth's atmosphere, it slows down and changes direction. When light travels through water, glass, or another medium it slows down even more, and changes direction again.

1. A. Use the text to define <u>refraction</u>.
   B. Explain the difference between reflection and refraction.

2. List at least two ways a medium can affect light. Cite evidence from the text to support your answers.

3. Why does light refract when it enters the Earth's atmosphere?

4. What does a straw appear to be bent when it enters a glass of water?

Make inferences from the text to determine whether or not each of the following is either a **cause** or **effect** of refraction.

_____ Light passes from space into the Earth's atmosphere.

_____ A pencil appears to bend in a glass of water.

_____ The curve of eyeglass lenses help some people to see better.

_____ Light changes speed and direction depending on the medium.

_____ Judging distance when swimming underwater is difficult.

Writing Prompt

Imagine you are trying to spear a fish for dinner. Write about what you see, and use the concept of <u>refraction</u> to explain why you should not aim your spear exactly where you see the fish.

Isaac Newton's Prisms

In 1665, Isaac Newton performed a famous experiment with a light and a prism. His discovery changed the way people thought about light. The following experiment is similar to the one performed in 1665.

Gather materials and follow the experiment procedure. Then answer the questions.

What you need:

- 1 prism (glass or plastic)
- 3 light sources (flashlight, laser pointer, and LED flashlight)
- 1 white index card

Procedure:

1. Secure the white index card to something so that it stands up.

2. Position the prism in front of the white index card.

3. Turn on the light source.

4. Shine the light through the prism onto the white index card.

5. Observe. Record your observations on the diagram.

Light

6. Repeat steps 3-5 using each light source.

1. What property of light does this experiment demonstrate?

2. What is the purpose of repeating the experiment with multiple light sources?

3. How did the results compare for each light source? Describe any similarities or differences.

4. What can you infer about the light produced by each light source?

Rainbows

Rainbows are colorful arches of light in the air. You can see them after a storm, or at the base of a waterfall. Rainbows form when light refracts through water droplets. The water droplets act like a prism, separating light into the visible spectrum of colors.

Rewrite each quotation to complete the chart. Use the completed chart to answer the questions.

Rainbow quotations:	What each quote means to me:
"Everyone wants happiness, no one wants the pain, but you can't make a rainbow without a little rain." — Unknown	
"My heart leaps up when I behold a rainbow in the sky." — William Wordsworth	
"May your journey through life be vibrant and full of colorful rainbows." — Harley King	

1. Identify a common theme among the quotations.

2. A. What does "rainbow" represent in the first quotation?
   B. What does "rain" represent in the first quotation?
   C. Is the use of "rain" and "rainbow" literal or figurative?

3. What can you infer about each author's perspective on rainbows?

4. In your opinion, do rainbows represent something positive or negative? Explain your answer.

5. Write your own quote using rainbows as an analogy for life.

Electromagnetic Spectrum

Look at the graphical data and answer the questions.

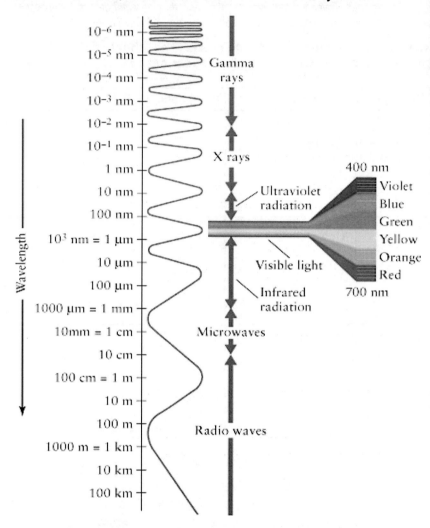

Km = kilometer
m = meter
cm = centimeter
mm = millimeter
um = micrometer
nm = nanometer

Conversion
1 inch = 2.54 centimeters

PART A: Analyze the graphical data to determine whether or each statement is **true** or **false**.

1. _____ The electromagnetic spectrum is mostly visible light.
2. _____ Microwaves have the smallest wavelength.
3. _____ Colors of visible light are divided by wavelength.
4. _____ Wavelengths on the electromagnetic spectrum are organized alphabetically.
5. _____ The range of 400nm to 700 nm are the only electromagnetic waves humans can see.

PART B: Make inferences from the graphical data to answer the questions.

6. Explain why light of wavelength 100 nm to 10 nm is called "ultraviolet."
7. If you measured your height with the longest microwave (10 cm), how many microwaves tall would you be?

PART C: Use the following chart to answer the questions.

8. What can you infer about the gray areas of the chart? What do the gray areas represent?
9. Which wavelengths of radio waves are most likely to penetrate the Earth's atmosphere—longer or shorter? Explain.
10. Which electromagnetic waves require microscopic measurement?

Wave type	Penetrates the Earth's atmosphere?	Approximate size of wavelength
Radio	Yes	Buildings
Microwave		Insects
	No	
Infrared	No	Pinpoint
Visible		Single cells
	Yes	
	No	
Ultraviolet	No	Molecules
X-ray	No	Atoms
Gamma Ray	No	Atomic nucleus

Infrared Radiation

Read the text and answer the questions.

We see visible light every day, but there are other forms of electromagnetic energy all around us we cannot see. One of these invisible energies is infrared radiation. The wavelength of infrared radiation is slightly longer than for visible light and shorter than for microwaves. The longest wavelength of infrared radiation is about the size of a pinhead. In contrast, the smallest infrared radiation wavelengths are as tiny as cells!

The human eye cannot see infrared radiation, but our skin can feel it! Longer wavelengths of infrared are called <u>thermal energy</u>— also known as heat! Infrared radiation from the sun is the warmth you feel on a hot day. Heat from other sources such as a fire, light bulb, or even hot concrete is infrared radiation, too.

Believe it or not, all living things produce infrared radiation, too—even you! Your body produces infrared radiation called "body heat." Humans cannot see infrared, but some animals can. The ability to see heat gives many predators an advantage. The snake, for example, can sense infrared. It uses this heat-seeking ability to hunt small rodents, even in dark holes.

Not all infrared wavelengths can be detected as heat. The shorter wavelengths of infrared radiation do not feel hot. In fact you cannot feel short wavelengths of infrared radiation at all! Many technological instruments use infrared radiation for communication. Your television remote probably uses this type of infrared light to communicate with your television.

1. A. Use the text to write a definition of <u>thermal energy</u>.
   B. What can you infer about using a thermostat and a thermometer from the root word "therm" in <u>thermal</u>?

2. Give two examples of heat you encountered today. Was the heat produced by infrared radiation? What was the source for each?

3. Can you infer that the temperature of objects that produce infrared radiation are warm or hot? Why or why not?

4. List at least three ways infrared radiation is useful to living things. Cite evidence from the text to support your response.

Concave & Convex Lenses

Read the text and answer the questions.

Lenses are made of curved transparent material, usually glass or plastic. A concave lens is usually used to spread light out, while a convex lens focuses light on a single point.

1. Use the text to label each of the following lenses.

_____lens   _____lens

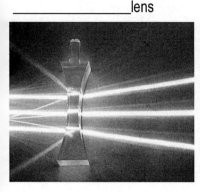
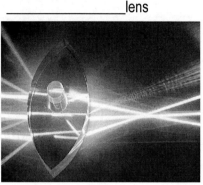

2. What part of the lens causes light to bend?

3. Complete the Venn diagram by comparing and contrasting the two images. Include lens shape, purpose, and effect on light.

Concave lens   **Convex lens**

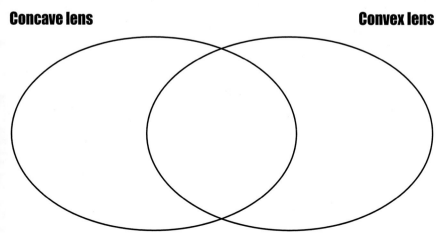

©Carole Marsh/Gallopade • www.gallopade.com • page 21

Light Poetry

Read the poem and answer the questions.

The Light of Love
by John Hay

1) Each shining light above us
    Has its own peculiar grace;
  But every light of heaven
    Is in my darling's face.

2) For it is like the sunlight,
    So strong and pure and warm,
  That folds all good and happy things,
    And guards from gloom and harm.

3) And it is like the moonlight,
    So holy and so calm;
  The rapt peace of a summer night,
    When soft winds die in balm.

4) And it is like the starlight;
    For, love her as I may,
  She dwells still lofty and serene
    In mystery far away.

1. What is the subject of the poem?

2. What type of literary device or style is used throughout the poem to describe the subject?

3. What is the subject of the poem compared to?

4. List the specific thing the subject is compared to in:
   A. Stanza 2
   B. Stanza 3
   C. Stanza 4

5. Use a word or phrase to summarize the characterization of how the subject is described in:
   A. Stanza 2
   B. Stanza 3
   C. Stanza 4

6. What can you infer about the author of the poem? Cite text from the poem to support your answer.

7. A. Circle all words in the poem that describe light.
   B. Based on the words you circled, what can you infer about the author's opinion of the subject? Explain.

8. In your opinion, what was the author's purpose for writing this poem? Explain your response.

Correlations to Common Core State Standards

For your convenience, correlations are listed page-by-page, and for the entire book!

This book is correlated to the Common Core State Standards for English Language Arts grades 3-8, and to Common Core State Standards for Literacy in History, Science, & Technological Subjects grades 6-8.

Correlations are highlighted in gray.

	READING	WRITING	LANGUAGE	SPEAKING & LISTENING
	Includes: RI: Reading Informational Text; RST: Reading Science & Technical Subjects	**Includes:** W: Writing; WHST: Writing History/Social Studies, Science, & Technical Subjects	**Includes:** L: Language; LF: Language Foundational Skills	**Includes:** SL: Speaking & Listening

PAGE #	RI / RST	W / WHST	L / LF	SL
2	1 2 3 4 5 6 7 8 9 10	1 2 3 4 5 6 7 8 9 10	1 2 3 4 5 6	1 2 3 4 5 6
3	1 2 3 4 5 6 7 8 9 10	1 2 3 4 5 6 7 8 9 10	1 2 3 4 5 6	1 2 3 4 5 6
4	1 2 3 4 5 6 7 8 9 10	1 2 3 4 5 6 7 8 9 10	1 2 3 4 5 6	1 2 3 4 5 6
5	1 2 3 4 5 6 7 8 9 10	1 2 3 4 5 6 7 8 9 10	1 2 3 4 5 6	1 2 3 4 5 6
6	1 2 3 4 5 6 7 8 9 10	1 2 3 4 5 6 7 8 9 10	1 2 3 4 5 6	1 2 3 4 5 6
7	1 2 3 4 5 6 7 8 9 10	1 2 3 4 5 6 7 8 9 10	1 2 3 4 5 6	1 2 3 4 5 6
8	1 2 3 4 5 6 7 8 9 10	1 2 3 4 5 6 7 8 9 10	1 2 3 4 5 6	1 2 3 4 5 6
9	1 2 3 4 5 6 7 8 9 10	1 2 3 4 5 6 7 8 9 10	1 2 3 4 5 6	1 2 3 4 5 6
10	1 2 3 4 5 6 7 8 9 10	1 2 3 4 5 6 7 8 9 10	1 2 3 4 5 6	1 2 3 4 5 6
11	1 2 3 4 5 6 7 8 9 10	1 2 3 4 5 6 7 8 9 10	1 2 3 4 5 6	1 2 3 4 5 6
12-13	1 2 3 4 5 6 7 8 9 10	1 2 3 4 5 6 7 8 9 10	1 2 3 4 5 6	1 2 3 4 5 6
14	1 2 3 4 5 6 7 8 9 10	1 2 3 4 5 6 7 8 9 10	1 2 3 4 5 6	1 2 3 4 5 6
15	1 2 3 4 5 6 7 8 9 10	1 2 3 4 5 6 7 8 9 10	1 2 3 4 5 6	1 2 3 4 5 6
16	1 2 3 4 5 6 7 8 9 10	1 2 3 4 5 6 7 8 9 10	1 2 3 4 5 6	1 2 3 4 5 6
17	1 2 3 4 5 6 7 8 9 10	1 2 3 4 5 6 7 8 9 10	1 2 3 4 5 6	1 2 3 4 5 6
18-19	1 2 3 4 5 6 7 8 9 10	1 2 3 4 5 6 7 8 9 10	1 2 3 4 5 6	1 2 3 4 5 6
20	1 2 3 4 5 6 7 8 9 10	1 2 3 4 5 6 7 8 9 10	1 2 3 4 5 6	1 2 3 4 5 6
21	1 2 3 4 5 6 7 8 9 10	1 2 3 4 5 6 7 8 9 10	1 2 3 4 5 6	1 2 3 4 5 6
22-23	1 2 3 4 5 6 7 8 9 10	1 2 3 4 5 6 7 8 9 10	1 2 3 4 5 6	1 2 3 4 5 6
COMPLETE BOOK	1 2 3 4 5 6 7 8 9 10	1 2 3 4 5 6 7 8 9 10	1 2 3 4 5 6	1 2 3 4 5 6

For the complete Common Core standard identifier, combine your grade + "." + letter code above + "." + number code above.

In addition to the correlations indicated here, the activities may be adapted or expanded to align to additional standards and to meet the diverse needs of your unique students!